TODAY'S DATE

I WOKE UP FEELING

IN THE AFTERNOON I FELT LIKE:

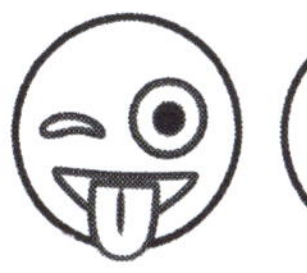

THE WEATHER WAS:

TODAY. . .

NIGHT TIME MOOD:

TODAY'S DATE

I WOKE UP FEELING

IN THE AFTERNOON I FELT LIKE:

THE WEATHER WAS:

TODAY. . .

NIGHT TIME MOOD:

TODAY'S DATE
TODAY'S THOUGHTS
TODAY'S WEATHER
TODAY'S MOODS
TODAY'S MEMORIES
I LOVE:

TODAY'S DATE
TODAY'S THOUGHTS
TODAY'S WEATHER
TODAY'S MOODS
TODAY'S MEMORIES
I LOVE:

TODAY'S DATE

I WOKE UP FEELING

IN THE AFTERNOON I FELT LIKE:

THE WEATHER WAS:

TODAY. . .

NIGHT TIME MOOD:

TODAY'S DATE

I WOKE UP FEELING

IN THE AFTERNOON I FELT LIKE:

THE WEATHER WAS:

TODAY. . .

NIGHT TIME MOOD:

TODAY'S DATE
TODAY'S THOUGHTS
TODAY'S WEATHER
TODAY'S MOODS
TODAY'S MEMORIES
I LOVE:

TODAY'S DATE
TODAY'S THOUGHTS
TODAY'S WEATHER
TODAY'S MOODS
TODAY'S MEMORIES
I LOVE:

TODAY'S DATE

I WOKE UP FEELING

IN THE AFTERNOON I FELT LIKE:

THE WEATHER WAS:

TODAY. . .

NIGHT TIME MOOD:

TODAY'S DATE

I WOKE UP FEELING

IN THE AFTERNOON I FELT LIKE:

THE WEATHER WAS:

TODAY. . .

NIGHT TIME MOOD:

TODAY'S DATE
TODAY'S THOUGHTS
TODAY'S WEATHER
TODAY'S MOODS
zZZ
TODAY'S MEMORIES
I LOVE:

TODAY'S DATE
TODAY'S THOUGHTS
TODAY'S WEATHER
TODAY'S MOODS
TODAY'S MEMORIES
I LOVE:

TODAY'S DATE

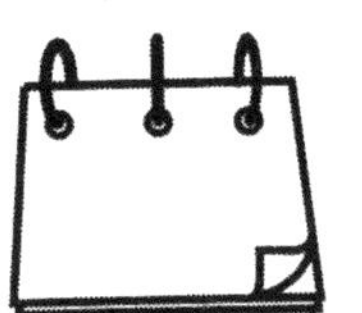

IN THE AFTERNOON I FELT LIKE:

THE WEATHER WAS:

TODAY. . .

NIGHT TIME MOOD:

TODAY'S DATE

I WOKE UP FEELING

IN THE AFTERNOON I FELT LIKE:

THE WEATHER WAS:

TODAY. . .

NIGHT TIME MOOD:

TODAY'S DATE
TODAY'S THOUGHTS
TODAY'S WEATHER
TODAY'S MOODS
TODAY'S MEMORIES
I LOVE:

TODAY'S DATE
TODAY'S THOUGHTS
TODAY'S WEATHER
TODAY'S MOODS
TODAY'S MEMORIES
I LOVE:

TODAY'S DATE

I WOKE UP FEELING

IN THE AFTERNOON I FELT LIKE:

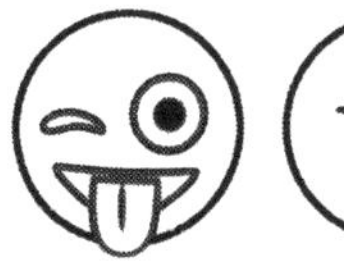

THE WEATHER WAS:

TODAY. . .

NIGHT TIME MOOD:

TODAY'S DATE

I WOKE UP FEELING

IN THE AFTERNOON I FELT LIKE:

THE WEATHER WAS:

TODAY. . .

NIGHT TIME MOOD:

TODAY'S DATE
TODAY'S THOUGHTS
TODAY'S WEATHER
TODAY'S MOODS
TODAY'S MEMORIES
I LOVE:

TODAY'S DATE
TODAY'S THOUGHTS
TODAY'S WEATHER
TODAY'S MOODS
TODAY'S MEMORIES
I LOVE:

TODAY'S DATE

IN THE AFTERNOON I FELT LIKE:

THE WEATHER WAS:

TODAY. . .

NIGHT TIME MOOD:

TODAY'S DATE

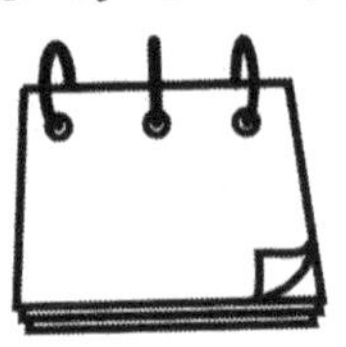

I WOKE UP FEELING

IN THE AFTERNOON I FELT LIKE:

THE WEATHER WAS:

TODAY. . .

NIGHT TIME MOOD:

TODAY'S DATE
TODAY'S THOUGHTS
TODAY'S WEATHER
TODAY'S MOODS
TODAY'S MEMORIES
I LOVE:

TODAY'S DATE
TODAY'S THOUGHTS
TODAY'S WEATHER
TODAY'S MOODS
TODAY'S MEMORIES
I LOVE:

TODAY'S DATE

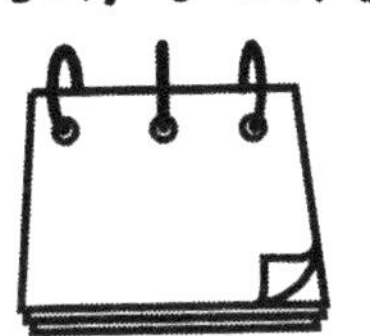

I WOKE UP FEELING

IN THE AFTERNOON I FELT LIKE:

THE WEATHER WAS:

TODAY. . .

NIGHT TIME MOOD:

TODAY'S DATE

I WOKE UP FEELING

IN THE AFTERNOON I FELT LIKE:

THE WEATHER WAS:

TODAY. . .

NIGHT TIME MOOD:

TODAY'S DATE
TODAY'S THOUGHTS
TODAY'S WEATHER
TODAY'S MOODS
TODAY'S MEMORIES
I LOVE:

TODAY'S DATE
TODAY'S THOUGHTS
TODAY'S WEATHER
TODAY'S MOODS
TODAY'S MEMORIES
I LOVE:

TODAY'S DATE

I WOKE UP FEELING

IN THE AFTERNOON I FELT LIKE:

THE WEATHER WAS:

TODAY. . .

NIGHT TIME MOOD:

TODAY'S DATE

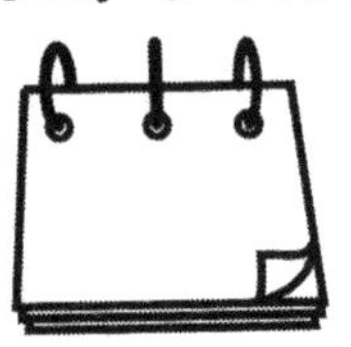

I WOKE UP FEELING

IN THE AFTERNOON I FELT LIKE:

THE WEATHER WAS:

TODAY. . .

NIGHT TIME MOOD:

TODAY'S DATE
TODAY'S THOUGHTS
TODAY'S WEATHER
TODAY'S MOODS
TODAY'S MEMORIES
I LOVE:

TODAY'S DATE
TODAY'S THOUGHTS
TODAY'S WEATHER
TODAY'S MOODS
TODAY'S MEMORIES
I LOVE:

TODAY'S DATE

I WOKE UP FEELING

IN THE AFTERNOON I FELT LIKE:

THE WEATHER WAS:

TODAY. . .

NIGHT TIME MOOD:

TODAY'S DATE

I WOKE UP FEELING

IN THE AFTERNOON I FELT LIKE:

THE WEATHER WAS:

TODAY. . .

NIGHT TIME MOOD:

TODAY'S DATE
TODAY'S THOUGHTS
TODAY'S WEATHER
TODAY'S MOODS
TODAY'S MEMORIES
I LOVE:

TODAY'S DATE
TODAY'S THOUGHTS
TODAY'S WEATHER
TODAY'S MOODS
TODAY'S MEMORIES
I LOVE:

TODAY'S DATE

I WOKE UP FEELING

IN THE AFTERNOON I FELT LIKE:

THE WEATHER WAS:

TODAY. . .

NIGHT TIME MOOD:

TODAY'S DATE

I WOKE UP FEELING

IN THE AFTERNOON I FELT LIKE:

THE WEATHER WAS:

TODAY. . .

NIGHT TIME MOOD:

TODAY'S DATE
TODAY'S THOUGHTS
TODAY'S WEATHER
TODAY'S MOODS
TODAY'S MEMORIES
I LOVE:

TODAY'S DATE
TODAY'S THOUGHTS
TODAY'S WEATHER
TODAY'S MOODS
TODAY'S MEMORIES
I LOVE:

TODAY'S DATE

IN THE AFTERNOON I FELT LIKE:

THE WEATHER WAS:

TODAY. . .

NIGHT TIME MOOD:

TODAY'S DATE

I WOKE UP FEELING

IN THE AFTERNOON I FELT LIKE:

THE WEATHER WAS:

TODAY. . .

NIGHT TIME MOOD:

TODAY'S DATE
TODAY'S THOUGHTS
TODAY'S WEATHER
TODAY'S MOODS
TODAY'S MEMORIES
I LOVE:

TODAY'S DATE
TODAY'S THOUGHTS
TODAY'S WEATHER
TODAY'S MOODS
TODAY'S MEMORIES
I LOVE:

TODAY'S DATE

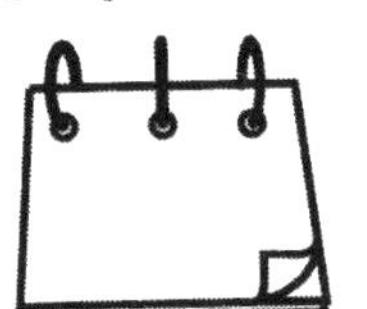

IN THE AFTERNOON I FELT LIKE:

TODAY. . .

NIGHT TIME MOOD:

TODAY'S DATE

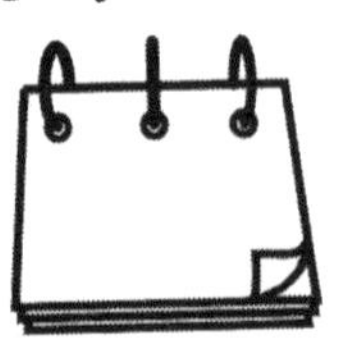

I WOKE UP FEELING

IN THE AFTERNOON I FELT LIKE:

THE WEATHER WAS:

TODAY. . .

NIGHT TIME MOOD:

TODAY'S DATE
TODAY'S THOUGHTS
TODAY'S WEATHER
TODAY'S MOODS
TODAY'S MEMORIES
I LOVE:

TODAY'S DATE
TODAY'S THOUGHTS
TODAY'S WEATHER
TODAY'S MOODS
TODAY'S MEMORIES
I LOVE:

I WOKE UP FEELING

TODAY'S DATE

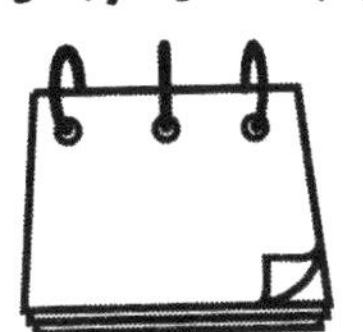

IN THE AFTERNOON I FELT LIKE:

THE WEATHER WAS:

TODAY. . .

NIGHT TIME MOOD:

TODAY'S DATE

I WOKE UP FEELING

IN THE AFTERNOON I FELT LIKE:

THE WEATHER WAS:

TODAY. . .

NIGHT TIME MOOD:

TODAY'S DATE
TODAY'S THOUGHTS
TODAY'S WEATHER
TODAY'S MOODS
TODAY'S MEMORIES
I LOVE:

TODAY'S DATE
TODAY'S THOUGHTS
TODAY'S WEATHER
TODAY'S MOODS
I LOVE:
TODAY'S MEMORIES

TODAY'S DATE

I WOKE UP FEELING

IN THE AFTERNOON I FELT LIKE:

THE WEATHER WAS:

TODAY. . .

NIGHT TIME MOOD:

TODAY'S DATE

I WOKE UP FEELING

IN THE AFTERNOON I FELT LIKE:

THE WEATHER WAS:

TODAY. . .

NIGHT TIME MOOD:

TODAY'S DATE
TODAY'S THOUGHTS
TODAY'S WEATHER
TODAY'S MOODS
TODAY'S MEMORIES
I LOVE:

TODAY'S DATE
TODAY'S THOUGHTS
TODAY'S WEATHER
TODAY'S MOODS
TODAY'S MEMORIES
I LOVE:

TODAY'S DATE

I WOKE UP FEELING

IN THE AFTERNOON I FELT LIKE:

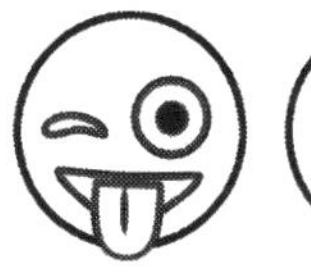  

THE WEATHER WAS:

TODAY. . .

NIGHT TIME MOOD:

TODAY'S DATE

I WOKE UP FEELING

IN THE AFTERNOON I FELT LIKE:

THE WEATHER WAS:

TODAY. . .

NIGHT TIME MOOD:

TODAY'S DATE
TODAY'S THOUGHTS
TODAY'S WEATHER
TODAY'S MOODS
TODAY'S MEMORIES
I LOVE:

TODAY'S DATE
TODAY'S THOUGHTS
TODAY'S WEATHER
TODAY'S MOODS
TODAY'S MEMORIES
I LOVE:

TODAY'S DATE

I WOKE UP FEELING

IN THE AFTERNOON I FELT LIKE:

THE WEATHER WAS:

TODAY. . .

NIGHT TIME MOOD:

TODAY'S DATE

I WOKE UP FEELING

IN THE AFTERNOON I FELT LIKE:

THE WEATHER WAS:

TODAY. . .

NIGHT TIME MOOD:

TODAY'S DATE
TODAY'S THOUGHTS
TODAY'S WEATHER
TODAY'S MOODS
TODAY'S MEMORIES
I LOVE:

TODAY'S DATE
TODAY'S THOUGHTS
TODAY'S WEATHER
TODAY'S MOODS
TODAY'S MEMORIES
I LOVE:

TODAY'S DATE

I WOKE UP FEELING

IN THE AFTERNOON I FELT LIKE:

THE WEATHER WAS:

TODAY. . .

NIGHT TIME MOOD:

TODAY'S DATE

I WOKE UP FEELING

IN THE AFTERNOON I FELT LIKE:

THE WEATHER WAS:

TODAY. . .

NIGHT TIME MOOD:

TODAY'S DATE
TODAY'S THOUGHTS
TODAY'S WEATHER
TODAY'S MOODS
TODAY'S MEMORIES
I LOVE:

TODAY'S DATE
TODAY'S THOUGHTS
TODAY'S WEATHER
TODAY'S MOODS
TODAY'S MEMORIES
I LOVE:

TODAY'S DATE

I WOKE UP FEELING

IN THE AFTERNOON I FELT LIKE:

THE WEATHER WAS:

TODAY. . .

NIGHT TIME MOOD:

TODAY'S DATE

I WOKE UP FEELING

IN THE AFTERNOON I FELT LIKE:

THE WEATHER WAS:

TODAY. . .

NIGHT TIME MOOD:

TODAY'S DATE
TODAY'S THOUGHTS
TODAY'S WEATHER
TODAY'S MOODS
TODAY'S MEMORIES
I LOVE:

TODAY'S DATE
TODAY'S THOUGHTS
TODAY'S WEATHER
TODAY'S MOODS
TODAY'S MEMORIES
I LOVE:

TODAY'S DATE

I WOKE UP FEELING

IN THE AFTERNOON I FELT LIKE:

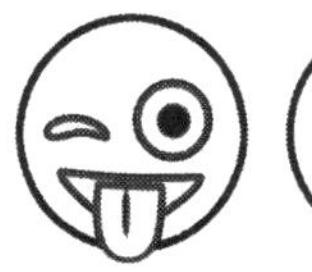 

THE WEATHER WAS:

TODAY. . .

NIGHT TIME MOOD:

TODAY'S DATE

I WOKE UP FEELING

IN THE AFTERNOON I FELT LIKE:

THE WEATHER WAS:

TODAY. . .

NIGHT TIME MOOD:

TODAY'S DATE
TODAY'S THOUGHTS
TODAY'S WEATHER
TODAY'S MOODS
TODAY'S MEMORIES
I LOVE:

TODAY'S DATE
TODAY'S THOUGHTS
TODAY'S WEATHER
TODAY'S MOODS
TODAY'S MEMORIES
I LOVE:

TODAY'S DATE

I WOKE UP FEELING

IN THE AFTERNOON I FELT LIKE:

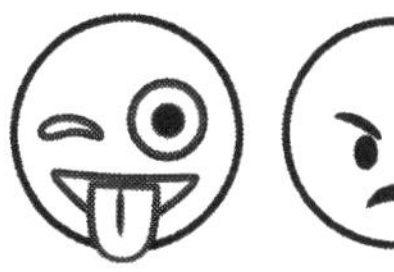

THE WEATHER WAS:

TODAY. . .

NIGHT TIME MOOD:

TODAY'S DATE

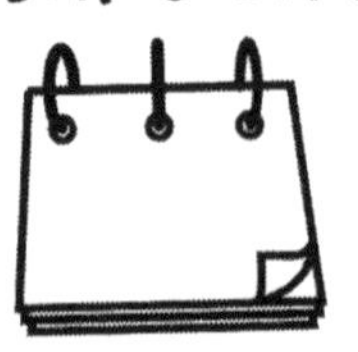

I WOKE UP FEELING

IN THE AFTERNOON I FELT LIKE:

THE WEATHER WAS:

TODAY. . .

NIGHT TIME MOOD:

TODAY'S DATE
TODAY'S THOUGHTS
TODAY'S WEATHER
TODAY'S MOODS
TODAY'S MEMORIES
I LOVE:

TODAY'S DATE
TODAY'S THOUGHTS
TODAY'S WEATHER
TODAY'S MOODS
TODAY'S MEMORIES
I LOVE:

TODAY'S DATE

I WOKE UP FEELING

IN THE AFTERNOON I FELT LIKE:

THE WEATHER WAS:

TODAY. . .

NIGHT TIME MOOD:

TODAY'S DATE

I WOKE UP FEELING

IN THE AFTERNOON I FELT LIKE:

THE WEATHER WAS:

TODAY. . .

NIGHT TIME MOOD:

TODAY'S DATE
TODAY'S THOUGHTS
TODAY'S WEATHER
TODAY'S MOODS
TODAY'S MEMORIES
I LOVE:

TODAY'S DATE
TODAY'S THOUGHTS
TODAY'S WEATHER
TODAY'S MOODS
TODAY'S MEMORIES
I LOVE:

TODAY'S DATE

I WOKE UP FEELING

IN THE AFTERNOON I FELT LIKE:

THE WEATHER WAS:

TODAY. . .

NIGHT TIME MOOD:

TODAY'S DATE

I WOKE UP FEELING

IN THE AFTERNOON I FELT LIKE:

THE WEATHER WAS:

TODAY. . .

NIGHT TIME MOOD:

TODAY'S DATE
TODAY'S THOUGHTS
TODAY'S WEATHER
TODAY'S MOODS
TODAY'S MEMORIES
I LOVE:

TODAY'S DATE
TODAY'S THOUGHTS
TODAY'S WEATHER
TODAY'S MOODS
TODAY'S MEMORIES
I LOVE:

TODAY'S DATE

I WOKE UP FEELING

IN THE AFTERNOON I FELT LIKE:

THE WEATHER WAS:

TODAY. . .

NIGHT TIME MOOD:

TODAY'S DATE

I WOKE UP FEELING

IN THE AFTERNOON I FELT LIKE:

THE WEATHER WAS:

TODAY. . .

NIGHT TIME MOOD:

TODAY'S DATE
TODAY'S THOUGHTS
TODAY'S WEATHER
TODAY'S MOODS
TODAY'S MEMORIES
I LOVE:

TODAY'S DATE
TODAY'S THOUGHTS
TODAY'S WEATHER
TODAY'S MOODS
TODAY'S MEMORIES
I LOVE:

TODAY'S DATE

I WOKE UP FEELING

IN THE AFTERNOON I FELT LIKE:

THE WEATHER WAS:

TODAY. . .

NIGHT TIME MOOD:

TODAY'S DATE

I WOKE UP FEELING

IN THE AFTERNOON I FELT LIKE:

THE WEATHER WAS:

TODAY. . .

NIGHT TIME MOOD:

TODAY'S DATE
TODAY'S THOUGHTS
TODAY'S WEATHER
TODAY'S MOODS
TODAY'S MEMORIES
I LOVE:

TODAY'S DATE
TODAY'S THOUGHTS
TODAY'S WEATHER
TODAY'S MOODS
TODAY'S MEMORIES
I LOVE:

TODAY'S DATE

I WOKE UP FEELING

IN THE AFTERNOON I FELT LIKE:

THE WEATHER WAS:

TODAY. . .

NIGHT TIME MOOD:

I WOKE UP FEELING

TODAY'S DATE

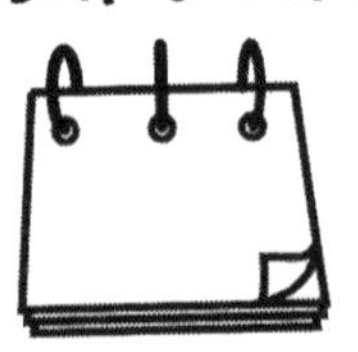

IN THE AFTERNOON I FELT LIKE:

THE WEATHER WAS:

TODAY. . .

NIGHT TIME MOOD:

TODAY'S DATE
TODAY'S THOUGHTS
TODAY'S WEATHER
TODAY'S MOODS
TODAY'S MEMORIES
I LOVE:

TODAY'S DATE
TODAY'S THOUGHTS
TODAY'S WEATHER
TODAY'S MOODS
TODAY'S MEMORIES
I LOVE:

TODAY'S DATE

I WOKE UP FEELING

IN THE AFTERNOON I FELT LIKE:

THE WEATHER WAS:

TODAY. . .

NIGHT TIME MOOD:

TODAY'S DATE

I WOKE UP FEELING

IN THE AFTERNOON I FELT LIKE:

THE WEATHER WAS:

TODAY. . .

NIGHT TIME MOOD:

TODAY'S DATE
TODAY'S THOUGHTS
TODAY'S WEATHER
TODAY'S MOODS
TODAY'S MEMORIES
I LOVE:

TODAY'S DATE
TODAY'S THOUGHTS
TODAY'S WEATHER
TODAY'S MOODS
TODAY'S MEMORIES
I LOVE:

TODAY'S DATE

I WOKE UP FEELING

IN THE AFTERNOON I FELT LIKE:

THE WEATHER WAS:

TODAY. . .

NIGHT TIME MOOD:

TODAY'S DATE
TODAY'S THOUGHTS
TODAY'S WEATHER
TODAY'S MOODS
TODAY'S MEMORIES
I LOVE:

Printed in Great Britain
by Amazon